Embracing Souls Series

Words of the Heart

By Jennifer Hillman

Abstract Illusions Media
Publishing Division
Jennifer Hillman, Inc.

Embracing Souls: Words of the Heart
By Jennifer Hillman

Published by Abstract Illusions Media
Division of Jennifer Hillman, Inc
PO Box 64370 Tucson, Arizona 85728
Orders:
abstractillusionsmedia@gmail.com

All rights reserved. No part of this book may be reproduced or transmitted in any form or by any means, electronic or mechanical, including photocopying, recording or any information storage and retrieval system, without written permission from the author, except for the inclusion of brief quotations in reviews.

Copyright Jennifer L. Hillman 2013
"Soul Mates" on cover ©Robert Holmes/Jennifer Hillman 2003
Abstract Illusions Media logo ©Jennifer Hillman 2013

ISBN electronic   097425391X

ISBN print ed 9780974253916

First Printing 2013
Printed in the United States of America

This book is dedicated to
everyone
who has passed or will be
passing through my journey.
Enjoy the adventure and bless the
people
who come into your life.

Table of Poetry

Foreword. Embracing Souls:
Words of the Heart   8
And then Night…   10
Soft Sounds of Love's
Embracing Chase   11
Sweet Savor of the Being   13
The Silence of the Unsaid   14
love simply be   15
Moment Be Moment 17
Touching Silence's Sweet Smile   19
Only Can I Smile   22
The Easy of the Comfort Zone   23
Wonders of Dancing Dreams   25
Midnight Mystery of the Hour   29
Maybe May   30
Chance with Sweet Dance   31
Bright Lights with Distance 32
Mind of Real & New Things Coming   33
Moon Smiling   35
Be Prudent and Wise 37
Touched   38
Rapture of Sweet Moment   39
Silence Be   40
Full Moon Embracing   41
Bright Dance with Distance 42
Building a House of Cards   43
Dance of Dances   45

Friends Made Moment's Smile 47
Allow the Dance of Exploration 48
Ah the Beloved and the Chase 49
Music Silence the Madness 50
Witness Within the Silence 52
Sweet Moon Kiss & Satin Ribbons 54
Warmth of the Friendship 55
As the Movement of Moment 59
Breathe and Be Reborn 60
Essence of the Morning Dew 62
How Damn Good Life Is 64
All Good Things in Time 70
Braze of the Midnight Sun 71
Shadows dance on the wall 72
Hunger Within the Moment's Caress 75
devotion music finds 77
Sparkles of the Night 79
Be-Ness 81
Spoon 83
As the Moments We Shared... 84
Awaken by Love 86
The Subtle Dreams Motions 88
How Many Ways 89
I, The Mirror 92
Acknowledgements: 95

Foreword.
Embracing Souls: Words of the Heart

Poetry is often the expression of love, of angst, of splendor, of the divine wisdom. Like the separation between self and spirit, source, the universe, it is only the limitation of the mind that end or begins with each breathe of reflection.
We all are one.
Words of the Heart is the continuing journey through Jennifer Hillman's poetry as she lives and becomes more aware of the values of the lessons she learns along the way. Her connection with the Divine is through the expression of relationships, near and far. The mysteries of life are only deepens and add more curious questions with each interactions with the soul mates on her journey. The lines blur the more open she becomes and embraces her creations and experiences.

Connection with Distance
Distance with Connection

Even with distance between
the people, the moment,
situation…
The impact of the connection can
move the soul; make the heart
beat strong, a person's world
change forever more…

<u>And then Night…</u>

A moment breathes
With things left unsaid
Though the undercurrent of emotions
Brings it out
Night

Bright sun lightens the loads
Clouds like marshmallow
Fluffy and sweet relief, feeling like a hug
And than
Night

Day be busy-ness and motion unending
The mind moving in many directions
but right
And then
Night
Yes,
Night.

Into to Day.
And the cycle continues breathing
With things left unsaid
Yet felt. …
Sigh.

Silence's Breath

Breath deepens
As heart beat quickens
Stars be close at hand
Time and space shifting
With the wisdom expanding
In the moment's Silence embraces

Touching soul and the heavens
above
Mirrors and truths dance
The wonderment of all the blessings
Connection close and far
With the wisdom expanding
In the moment's Silence whispers

Breeze of coolness
Warmth of love sweet nectar
Movement among the night
Ever present and enchanting
With the wisdom expanding
In the moment's Silence expresses

Be one with me, myself and I
And all that is alive and daring
Oneness comes to me
In a vision, touch and breathe
With the wisdom expanding
In the moment's Silence smiles.

Soft Sounds of Love's Embracing Chase

Soft song echoes in my mind
As the soft touch of love strokes my cheek
Silent words of promises
The interlude of fantasy and life
Whispering friendly gestures
And peeling back the layers of hurt

Soft song continues in my mind
As a reminder of love's sweetness to the soul
Opening the heart to this nectar
In longing embrace
Silent words of maybes
Delays are easily made
And peeling back the layers of pain

Soft song brings my mind to calm
As the strength of love's sweetness grows
Opening the door of possibilities
In distant dance of wonder
Silent words of longing
Impatience is born
And peeling back the layers of joy

Oh the sweet sounds and gentle touches
Within the mind and heart
Friendships can open and close the door
In the chaos of time and being
Silent words of passion's teases
No more excuses making
And peeling back the layers of doubt

Into the delicate hellos and hugs combine.

Sweet Savor of the Being

S*weet savor of the moment's embrace*
A kind of kiss … of sorts
Touching the wondering of the heart
Tenderly gingerly wanting…
Stop the breath
Time lingers
Why…
Question deepen
With the angst of wind thickens
Smiling with release
Expectations dropped
With words and actions
Being be
Oh Be

Oh sweet surrender to the soul
Savory dance and sassy moves
Embracing the taste of passionate caress
Of the oneness in the truth
Soothing the heart and breathe deepens

Oh yes…
Time continues to linger
With the gentle touch of pleasure
Feeling the smoothness of skin
Enwrapping the moment in golden amber
Connection be…
Complete and again…
Oh so sweet smile upon the face.
Sigh…

The Silence of the Unsaid

Sweeping embrace of emotions and feelings
Felt intensely yet lying beneath the truth.
Surface expression
With the silence dancing
With the interlude of the moment's breath
Of intentions known yet left unsaid.

Dangling in the breeze
Dawning of the presence
Deep impressions reeling high
Yet they are dreams of dreams
Truth of secrets reveals and wondering

In the silence of unsaid moments
Felt so intensely
Vision heighten with anticipations
Yet expectations dropped.
Learned motions of words and actions
Fears understood
In the silence of the unsaid.
Unsaid yet so deeply felt…
Patience grows with the release
Of the silence of the unsaid…
Being said.

love simply be

And then the whisper came…
The secrets of my soul
Lingered and spilled
Like blood from a bullet to the heart
All hidden from myself
Came pouring out
Like an avalanche of silence…

Be

I sat in the stillness
With the darkness of my soul and…
Listen
Witnessed
Simply be…
Be
Present…
Accountable and responsive for all
The undoings of my journey
The decay
Released…
Past
Present
And Lord knows…
It was I
&
"I" died.
Forming into a speck
On the leaf
Of the might oak
And
Simply be

Be

What more of nothingness?
The emptiness
Grows…

Into the overwhelm essence of
Love
Joyful tears filled the vast universe of
Stars Moons and Suns…
Simply be
BE
Just Be.
*Breathe with ease…**BE**.*

Moment Be Moment

Whispering sunshine smile deep
Moment be moment
Not more?
Breathe more deeply
No more of …

Heart beat
Knocking
No more of…
Well…
Maybe…
Right?

Whispering moonlit dance deep
Embracing moment be moment
Kiss.
No more of…
No more.
Hmmm.

Water lapping
Well…
No more of…
No more.
Right?

Smiles deep
Talk is cheap
Actions tell true.
Moment be moment
And all is what it is…
Moment be moment
No more of…

No more.
Maybe…
Be telling.
Be wise.
Silence deepening the caress…
Right?

Touching Silence's Sweet Smile

Touching smile
Within and bring it into the light
And dance among the stars.
Silent prayers
Delicate words of wisdom
Just returned
Blessings of heavens

Sweet kiss of liberation
Tender moment of reverence
Of understanding and presence
Brings the heart to center
And joy fills your life.
Be kind with the look and
Gentle with awakening.
Others be who they are
In the place and space for them

Embracing the kiss of the sun's sweet touch
Upon the cheek and be free
As life is what it is
And that is just fine.

Share a smile and words of laughter
Can be a friend back to center;
And you to a place
Of sweet kiss of freedom and bliss.
Uniting the heart and soul with one.
Brilliance in the mundane, as love is within all.
Taking the breath away
As the breeze sooths against your skin,
Whispering the presence of that love's embrace.

***You Know*...**

You know
when you think
you know
what you know
and yet do you?

Do you really know
what you think
you know
or is that part of the illusion?

A part of the dream
within the dream to think
you know
what you know?

The more you think
you know
why you do
you know
what you think
you know
then the why
you know
you think
isn't the why at all?

Know yourself is
just knowing
what you know
of yourself.

The patterns
and actions
and such knowingness
that knowing that
it isn't worth
what you knowing
what and why you think
you know at all.

So if you don't know
what you know
and don't deny that
you don't know
and knowing this
you know
what and why
you don't know.
Right?

Only Can I Smile

Only can I smile while I
Focus on the energy ball rolling my hands
Or the energy slinky bouncing in the air
Free flowing energy and abundant fun about
Like love I feel as I connect to my heart
Peaceful bliss and slight smile appears
The knowingness and joy that lights up in my being

The Master's energy fills my heart and eyes
With tears
Humble express of the trueness pure presence
As I feel my true self rise up from the depths
Whisper the secrets and wisdom of the ages
Dear Child, Dear Child…
Sweet hugs and embraces
Of the heart's true essence

Only can I smile
With the warmth inside
To the point of tears and laughter releasing
All the silliness of worries and pointless questions
Wise to question, yet repeat the question
Repeat the lesson twice more.

Only can I smile with the joyous embrace
Deep inside,
Only can I smile.

The Easy of the Comfort Zone

Within the journey of the soul
The ways of the ego find the ways of a smile
The ins and outs of deception
Compromising the truth
Of the moment
For the easy of the comfort zone

When fears are deepest
And darkness can fall upon you
The bidding of the dark night of the soul approaching
One can sense the inevitable descend
As the ego works to make peace
Creating the easy
Of the comfort zone

When it feels too good and things do flow
One can guess that it will go
The build up of the ego's walls
Make the darkness ever deeper
Masking the reality
Of what one is doing
For the easy of the comfort zone

The ego makes it so easy
To find what you need to bring the peace
Of the fears and insecurities
Without doing the true work
Of the soul
Accepting one's flaw is all good
Resisting the change
Only deepen the hole

Gurus are here to help us grow
Not to make excuses to let go
Of the work that is needed
By making perceptions to fit the ego
The master have done their work
Not through the easy
Of the comfort zone

Now is the time to face those fears
Understanding them
And embrace them
Not through escapism and deception
Through the ego.

<u>Wonders of Dancing Dreams</u>

Dancing stars across the sky
Whispers lingers in the mind
As dreams live and be as one
In the early morning of the times.

Wondering, pondering
Magic happens
With the clearing of disbelief
Removing the blocks
So deeply hindering.

Moment of motion is upon us
With the truth and the notions
Touching fingertips
Through moon dust
Bringing the trust one longs to find.

Maharishi's Whispers

Liberation comes from acceptance of all flaws
by facing the fears of the flaws and only when one faces the fear that is a flaw will one truly be truly free from the mind and "I" of the mind, within the sacred unity of the soul and the oneness.
Trusting oneself is also gaining from facing the flaws of the illusionary fears holding one from truly existing in liberation.
Liberation brings the freedom into the peaceful place that will bring one to a greater understanding and it starts with one question to be asked of oneself.
Inquiring into the depths of your fears that linger and like a weight or burden hold you in place while you see the mind dancing with the endless thoughts and anxiety.

Liberation comes from acceptance
Of the flaws and inconsistency
Looking at one's fears and the illusions
Releasing the power of the mind of "I"
To embrace the heart's true whispers
Trusting self and inquiring deeper
Surrendering to the Guru and Master
To purify and bring the peace

With the time and space of now
And live your life as you wish

So much unsaid and felt between
The silence and the stillness lingering
Love and friendship, the bond of the souls
Can heal and aid in relations of the mirror
With the self and understandings

The teacher can pull you into the chaos
Only as the means to bring you closer
To the truth of self and the liberation's breathing
Through the silence and words whispering
To open communication with your soul

Feel the Guru and the Master
As their smile bring you home…
To that peace of mind through acceptance
Know that you're truly home
Through the understanding of one's soul.

**Embracing Galaxy of Dreams**

Nighttime dance,
Mingling through dreams
Soft words of support
Gained in starlight's glancing
Fingertips touching
Waiting for the galaxy's showing
The smiles and whispers hiding
in distance chances

Waiting for the galaxy of wishes
To bring dreams of meeting
in full moon lighting
Music within the heart unites until then
Lapping waters embracing
Warmth of the silence looks and caresses
Mingling through the dreams
Of the nighttime dance.

Midnight Mystery of the Hour

It comes the time around
midnight
or a bit later
A voice familiar and gently speaking
Lips moving in whisper, yet I don't
hear
Things unsaid yet I feel it clear
Connection and presence
Essence so dear

Friendship's growing and distance
still
Words said, in play and jest
Stories changing, twisted and much
Nothing personal, yet from the heart
The connection of the midnight hour

Fingers holding tight and weaved
Eyes embracing in sensual greed
Lips moving yet nothing said
Only felt in my mind's eye and heart
As time is moving fast and far

Life lived yet missing
Puzzle pieces falling
Space and intentions
Agreements and timing
Heavens move earth
Yet it all be still.

Maybe May

Maybe May will bring to light The whispering wisdoms to heart
Expressing and releasing things Opening up to the reception Of the silence and dance of life Accepting things as they come
Being patience as one can.

Understand the game of patience
Being true and fearless
Presence and being real
To the friends who still touch my soul
As all is reveals as it is needed
Rejoice in the new month arrival
Open arms and dance in light

Enjoy, my friends with a big smile.

Chance with Sweet Dance

Night Dream Fade as the sun awakens
Smiles deep heart pure
As the dance of the night dwells and lingers
Just a moment longer...
Tenderness to the soul
Interlocking fingers of hope and knowing
Patience be a friend, an ally and lesson

Looking the morning twilight
There is no distance between us here
Galaxy looks within my heart
Fills me with a gentle kiss upon my mind
Moment be as it is
Created for a reason
Make peace with the hmm

Sipping tea and embracing oneness
Willow tree dances
As the breeze continues
Whispering and singing sweet songs
Music lingers and awakens imagination's child
Creation of acceptance and allowing
The unfolding of life's grand plan
Taking a chance and dance
In wholeness of now
Change can come and always does.

Bright Lights with Distance

Bright lights of the city
And a look in your eyes
Telling signs of things to come
Wisdom says be still in the mind
Alone with one's thoughts of nothing

Breathe in the moment
Live life as tomorrow is your last.

Dance of distances
Words and notions
Real yet hmm…
Still good friends indeed.
So much unsaid, felt deeply
Wishing more were said
Accepting the lessons and letting things be

In the stillness of the night
Your wandering enter, stirring my mind
With your wondering
Connection deep, yet not
Limitations placed in line but by whom?
Be fear or luck… does it matter?

City of Lights,
Our adventures waiting
And all is divine.

Mind of Real & New Things Coming

Mind goes quiet now and then…
More so now with the release
Of a thought and a notion
Of a dream and a suggestion
Heart be still and quite active

Full Moon dancing
Expression quickly
As new life begin
Explore the adventure
With open eyes and wisdom home
The patterns broken, changing
and/or vanished

Took the step by step by step
Took one's hand and show the light
Friendship grows
In what direction is now unknown
Heart connection still presence
Yet distance lingers and makes me …
Time is now
With appreciation great
Of the hearts and souls
Be something else
Fears may come and make
appearance
Give them a kiss and be quite clear

I love this journey
And see the illusions
Communication and perceptions may
differ

The heart of connections
True friends will remain
When words spoken are true in
action

Real is real
Illusion is such
Joy and love is what it is
The focus of the moment now
With a hug and a moment to listen
And to hear…

The whispers of the other's dreams
And be good cheer
Be real with Self
And I see now
All I have learned
And be grateful for.

Moon Smiling

Paleness of the skies
The brightness within
Smiles illuminate the moments
Of sublime
Telling the sweetness of a friendship
dear nectar ~The liqueur

Embracing the moonlight
And dawning moment
In breath and smile
Bright light shining
Upon my face and presence
As my heartbeat quickens
With truth and trust in the essence

Releasing the old and understood
Adventure bring the new
With passion and new wisdom
Of living the now and ever knowing
The heart connections are blessings

Be Real and Honest
With Self and Others
Opens the door to communication
End the twisted stories that can cause
Misunderstandings and Misaligning
Of heart's own beat and life being.

Smile at the moon
And wink at the moment
Knowing the moment is grand
As the days of happiness grow
With the light of passion
Embraced and shared.

Lilies Danced

Lilies danced
Fingertips kissed
Wondering dreams
And heart-string lips
Passion rises among the stars
As the moon fades, wading and such

Tell the tales
Friendships being
Twisting like the willow trees
Silence yet with music whispers
Nuance and rhetoric flames

Presence thought
Untouched by choice
Turned to find the missing
The heart-string lips quiver
Quieted to hear the unsaid said

Time passes
Heals the said
Mistakes and well…
Humans are human
Be what they will.

Be Prudent and Wise

Be prudent and wise
Contradict and surrender
With all the understandings
And presence bound
Stop now and listen…

Listen to the whistling tree
The hawk cries and flies low
Be firm and don't hold your breath
Time … your time be close at hand.
Not reason to continue
Let go and be just my essence
The shadow of shadow's breeze
Allow the truth to flow and go home
Inside the mind's eye and silence calls

Home bound oh yes indeed.
Love be following me
Me knowing the truth
Between spoken word and jest.
Action dormant and filled with angst
Power moves and thought chaos
Done with the game
And rest be my friend.

Touched

Touched…
Heart soften deep
Lingering promises
Pieces found
Others released
Holding oneself and breathing in

Sight of love
Friendships die and reborn
Essence of truth
Insights lighten
Soften the moments' tears
Smile gained

Understanding loss
Or near loss
Recovery… perhaps
Change changed
Breeze whispers
Raindrops dancing

Choices made
Changed
Redesigned refined
Fabric torn
Sewn
Still… well, maybe.

__Rapture of Sweet Moment__

Rapture of the moment
Breath and beauty blend
Nature's sweet nectar
Tender touch and vision
Peace and balance at its best
Wind swept tears embraced.

Depth of presence
Friendships lingering near
Distant in physical
Not from my heart and
Sense of dreams
Hugs and smiles…

With questions and talk
Among the stars and gentle breeze
Water quick and seldom dark
Caress the silence
In look and dance
Patience be relieved

Prayers be answered
Released from the past
Love be in the inhale
Light be in the exhale
Understanding of the wanderings
All in the rapture of the moment's
sweet kiss.

<u>Silence Be</u>

Silence…
Touched in radiance being
Be…
Still and breath
Intangibility paradox smiles
Soften words of wondering

Question asked…
Pondered
Be…
Light of heart
Humor of presence
Look…feel breath

Touch of hand
Eyes unite
Be…
First glance
Release doubt
Hug the moments sorrow

Smiling prance
Answers in silent
Be…
Think too much
No more
Understand first be right
Breathe…

Full Moon Embracing

The clouds danced as the moon blazed.
Whispering the mysteries
Into the late night air
Steeples reached to touch the stars
As the Silence only smiled as a dare

Peaceful wonder in the moment
Of delight inspiration of creation
Being more and more into the heart
Of expression of the mind

Brilliance of the bright moon light
Like the soul who witness this moment
Be at rest and do what feels
The trusting of oneself and making it real

To touch the moon of silver and dust
Like tasting love for the first time
Embracing the eyes with a single glance
As if tomorrow will never come.

Bright Dance with Distance

Bright lights of the city
And a look in your eyes
Telling signs of things to come
Wisdom says be still in the mind
Alone with one's thoughts of nothing

Breathe in the moment
Live life as tomorrow is your last.
Dance of distances
Words and notions
Real yet …
Still good friends indeed.
So much unsaid, felt deeply
Wishing more were said
Accepting the lessons and letting
things be

In the stillness of the night
Your wandering enter, stirring my
mind
With your wondering
Connection deep, yet not
Limitations placed in line but by
whom?
Be fear or luck… does it matter?

City of Lights, our adventures
waiting
And all is divine.

Building a House of Cards

Building a house out of cards
With little truth and flimsy structure
The dance of words and realizations
Passionate exchanges and hopeless strategies
From the mind and ego's pride
Leaving your heart to wonder aimlessly
The winds and rains will come
Blowing the truth into your face
Of how you made yet another choice
Leading you to trip yourself
Causing clouds to cover your sunshine
As the thunder roars in the distance,
And coming your way.
If you don't have sunshine shining in your life
And you know where your sunshine is
Ego and pride stopping you from connection
Of the thought of your mind
Telling you what must do this
Delaying and blocking your sun's breath of truth from shining
Only adds to the hard lessons of life
You stopping you truly living
And slowly dimming the dreams of your heart's sun
It will likely bringing in another storm after another storm
When you know you can leave
It is your ego that will bring you down
To your knee

As the water raising around you
As you do what you do to other's
appease
Until you can't do it anymore
Surrendering to the truth
Of what you have done
Think twice before you died
Of the wisdom you have gain

As you surely will come back again
And the Universe will remind you
Of the gift of sunshine
With honey sweet dreams
And you let your ego get greedy
For the pipe dreams of others
Turning away from your gut feelings
And intuition you resisted.
All for what creation is your game?
You create your life's lessons
The house that you live
Make it in faith, truth and trust
You will have all you need
Let the ego have it way
Only the storms will know your
name.

Dance of Dances

Dance of dances
We do it well…
Three steps together
Side step four
Turn and twist…
And face each other again
Mélange to distance
Consistent pattern of this we must agree
Music changes, movement hasn't

The interplay of the dance
The passion shared
With promise and descend
So attracted, yet detaching
Look within the words you say
Play the game once more and again.
Turning and playing
Yet pull each other in again
You step right in denial
Apologize on cue
A moment of dramatic silence to enhance
Time to take a breath, regroup
And change the music.
You turn and be left of me
With a smile and hand on hand
Push me out and twist me around
I am dizzy from this dance
Though somehow enjoy it all
How? I truly don't know.

You seem to be in the lead
I follow along
Yet I know the steps

Before you move your feet.
Pattern of this dance consistent
indeed
The music may change
Heartbeat has only deepens

Words snap with passion
Mania continues
Dance becomes heated
Distraction of pleasure
Not a bad thing or is it?
Friendship bond
With safety net attached and needed.

Friends Made Moment's Smile

Within a moment's smile, a lifetime can live.
Connection of friendship can remain or come and go
The heart connection is open
Even no matter where each goes
Friends are friends if both agree

Magic happens every moment you breathe
Allow the truth of who you are to be reveal
Within the magic, the intertwining
Of fingers dance
Feeling the pulse of each others space

Honest reflection in dreams and fears
Brings reality into what is real
Resistance and projection may be a part
Though with discernment
One can tell the variant

Mirrors of mirror
Let it all be fine with knowing each be unique
Once the mirror is broken
Different realities may form

Appreciation of the moment's smile
The music and understanding being gained
Connection within heart's space is there

What it is and what we make of it now.
Be true to you and all you be.

Allow the Dance of Exploration

Dance, wind chimes in my mind
Breeze blow and frees me
Brings me back to heart
Listening into the wisdom seen
Friends echo love and peace
Knowing truth, trust and being

Allowing the mixture into the food
Tasting the variety of the times
Sipping the flavors of life's desires
Exploring divine essences of the sublime
Laughter brings release
Of tension's harm
As the smile breaks loose
With delightful wonders
And heart felt moments.

Ah the Beloved and the Chase

Ah the Beloved and the Chase
Need not be hard nor fast
Release and surrender
> *To that moment of passion*

Embrace the truth of what life really is
Limitations of the mind hinder the dance
Of the sweetness of nectar
With honey drizzled
In rapture of the moment first taste
> *Be divine*

And have all the world's compassion
When weak knee be sublime.
Ah the Beloved and the Chase
Chase be light and filled
> *With the love of heart*

Balance the mind, spirit and heart
Be whole and complete while on your way
Journey into self and truths come in time
As the dance continues on
With the promise of wisdom
Open heart and knowing
> *No more than before.*

Music Silence the Madness

Music silence the madness in this moment
Mirrors be cleared and cleaned with respect
Insights may seem harsh
with the cutting edge
of forgiveness
sharpen
my mind be
on overload and overwhelm
with simple presence of a friend
reality be snap
hold nothing for nothing is real
hold you in close as I wish you well
know this dance is not over
timing is what it is
fear and denial can be a bitch
on one's smile.
close connection and completion be near
exploration has consequences
someday we all pay that price
I can only hope it isn't too much to bear.

Compassion Be More Than A Moment

Compassion be more than a
moment's thought
A mood or a feeling
Hints it lives deep in part
It grows within the heart
Through hard lessons
Of being, doing and seeing
Of others and their journey choices
Emerging and among the stars of
Heaven
Breathing in the magic of Sirius
Dancing, Dancing
Oh heart of Light

Come to me
Come
And let us be merry
Raise glasses of wine
And Laughter so high
That all the world looks
To see the splendor
Joyous reverence of friends
So near and far from us.
Bring sol

Witness Within the Silence

Within the Silence
The moon of you sings to me
Whispering words unspoken
And felt so deeply
Connection real
Within the dreamscape being
Midnight visitations continue
I be your witness as you go along
Here in the Silence
Know my heart beat is
One with yours.

Thoughts and reactions
The dance of truth and the ego
Lingering elements
Of the moment's choices
And lessons in learning
Reach into the deep of the darkness
In the sleep time of passions…
All is reveal
Within the Silence of being

Focusing on the now moment and presence
We be what we are for each other
More than we can be,
Yet unique in the motion
Honey-kissed passions and Deserving of the best
We go to the places of warm sunshine and blessings
The Silence brings
Dreams into reality
As patience plays along

Divine being presence
And holding tight
In the whispers.

Sweet Moon Kiss & Satin Ribbons

Sweet kiss of the near full moon
Upon my cheek
As I sit under the stars
Gazing at the galaxy brazing above
Dreams of the moment
Embracing the blessings
Of this peace and inspiration
Of my heart

Sharing a sip of wine
With music's charm
Holding the whispers in my mind
As the words rambling
Onto the page
Oh sweet tender Luna
Swim under the illumination's arms
Knowing the truth is revealed
 in time

Heartbeat dance in time with the tune
Slow and simply in step
With the moon
Flow into the river of the ribbons
Brightly colored and satin slick
Wrap the connection
Of soul and heart

With love of myself continuing
To deepen
Appreciate as I let go of delusions
I am heading home soon indeed
I am heading
Where I belong soon enough
Being in the place
My heart stillness lingers.

Wishing well all friends
Along my journey.

__Warmth of the Friendship__

Brilliance within the darkness
Essence born again through truth's death
Holds the reality at bay
Acceptance and allowing the dream live
With the unspoken loudly screams

I smile
I cry
I be
I smile

And laugh at the humor of the game played
So much drama and for what?
Ah, the sweet tenderness shared.

Now I send magic as I create possibilities
Into the wisdom and reconnection of being
It was all the ego's game
Controlling
Or seemingly wanting control
Through the limitation
Of the fear and insecurity of the reality
All illusions.

And the better man wins
And I will dance in the rain
In the splendor of the celebration
In the warmth of the sun
Waves of gratitude for the friendship's depth

Respect of the inner knowingness of the unknown born again.

Drift, Stray, Move to Be

Drift into
Drift away
Drift like….

Love's embrace surrounds and aloof
Heart open, dancing in the rain
Tasting the sweetness of the soul
Honey-kissed and wine arousing
pleasure
Touching the inner being of the
blissful moment
Essences of you and I
Oh be so entangled and intertwining
magic
Resistance endured as the fears
realized
Humor the time of learning through
exploring
What present and in sight
Yet none fulfills the empty void as
one may have thought
Fill the time with work and talk
The shallowness takes hold and
repulsive
Depth craving of freedom and
liberation
From the self in deepest connection

Stray into
Stray away
Stray like…

Roaming vagabonds
Here and there ~ just being
Heart open, dancing in the sun rays
of life
Warmth feels good, yet empty still
A piece gone missing to fulfill this
adventure
Is it just in the mind or really gone…
The fear of death or is it really?
Ego's strokes the thoughts of worry
Be with the wanderer within me still
Always looking and looking for more.

Move into
Move away
Move like…

The soul into the understanding
now
The truth of the connection with you
and I
Friendship deep and love enduring
The games that life does play
Divine inspired to move us closer
To our true selves with caressing
embers
The fire within yet burning
Slow and steady
Breathe of truth lingers
Within the silence of our hearts
Being one now and always.

As the Movement of Moment

As the movement and rhythms
of moment's dance
The breathe and ease
of the beauty within
Grace the hearts everlasting
splendors;
Feeling and experiencing the fullness
of life.

Embrace it all, dear child of love.
Know that it is all real
And still the illusion
Of your imagination gone wild.
Fully presence in the essence of
mind.

Wild and wondrous…
Oh dance oh dance child
With the music in heart
The universe's orchestra is here
And fully charmed.
Move in the breath
And the grace that you are.
Be fully presence
And know who you are.

Brilliance, magical and everything
else…
Dance with the essence out of mind
Embrace yourself and love…
And all be divine.

___Breathe and Be Reborn___

Breathe and Be Reborn
Into the Lightness
Of your Heart and Inner Truths.
Speak…
in the Silence of Dreams,
Knowing the words
Bring the peace into your Soul.
Radiant the Love that is your True
Self and Again...
Be Reborn.
Reflections of the Shadow's Dance,
The Music Comes Alive
Within the wind and moonbeam light
                    streaming
Into the River deep
Full of the essence of the inner
dwelling and peaceful bliss
Caress and embrace the sweetest of
moments
Ah, be one again
Without mistake nor doubt
Feel the passion's awakening as you
dance,
Express the elegance of your soul
Doubt not the reasons
for your space.
Listen deeply to the whispers
Of the inner dreaming stars of bright
New Moon be silent, dark
And hearing your whispers
Touch the heavens and drink upon
the wine of Angels
Seen before you…
Dance and be as one

The Beloved

Fool not
By your mind's confusion
And ego's games of past
Rejoice in the innocence
Of the heart sweetness.
Purity of heart brings the inner
child to play
Accept all the aspects to live
With care and confidence.
Be the freedom you long to share
Be the love you are
And simply be the truth
Of who you are.
YOU.

Essence of the Morning Dew

Dew essence of the morning light
Haste not the reality of love
       and powers be.
Holding tight
       to the moment's breath
To release the very best to thee
Focus rightly in as all just is
Knowing truth is revealed
Peeled away and see inside
The heart of all be it now
Blessings surround
       as lessons learned
Respect the choices and be at peace

Ah the joy and happiness expand
With the centering and reverence
       of the stars
Peace and receiving
all that is needed
With the growing
       of the smile's meeting
Music plays in Silence's realm
Bring more to me the less I require
Nothing be real, yet all is
       Exactly as we all created
Knowing this is for the highest good
The dance of friendships continues
New faces and places
Renewing passions
       in dreams of the heart
All be true and in the essence
       of morning dew.

Balance of the Human

Balance of the heart and mind
Balance of the be and do
Balance in the seeing and feeling
Balance in Trust…
and Question
One comes to a point that it is alright
It's just what it is for now
And in another moment, another breath
A smile with wondering what happens the next
Or does it really?
The games and drama
All for entertainment
The balancing of the strife and boredom,
Yet at what expense and cost to you?
And is it all really worth in the end?
Do you just let go and let it be?
The dance between ugliness and beauty Ego and Love One is illusion and one is truth Friendship, Enemies or what?
It is either or… maybe that center of balance,
Right?
The gray matter gains little
As the blending commences
Yet many play and claim to be in that space
You walk it or you just talk it
That is the truth of what is it
What it is?

Balancing between the fine line
Balance of black and white
Balance of peace and chaos
Balance of Love and Hate
Passions enduring essence in
balance.

How Damn Good Life Is

Your heart opens for the first time
With the sight of this...
And you breathe in deep
And stop breathing
At the same time

Time just stopped
The moment has become
More than more
Love hits hard

When you are open to the mystery
Of the life surrounding you.
Freedom comes flooding in
And you realized
How damn good life is

Smile your face
And you can't explain why
You don't have to... people feel it
Leaping out of you...
Oh that sweet loving confidence and
You are doing just fine

When you are open to the mystery
Of the life loving you.
Miracles come flooding in
And you realized
How damn good life is

Dance in your step
No music around
And you don't care
With the great tune within
The heart beat strong and loud
You are finding
Just how life is profound
You are doing just fine.

When you are open to the mystery

Of the life embracing you.
Miracles come flooding in
And you realized
How damn good life is

Smile at the Dance

Smile as the thoughts drift through
the mind
as the uncertainty comes and sit to
visit
grazing with wide eyes wonderment
as its guide
the truth reveals as the time stops
within the breathe of love
Nothing is permanent,
except the connections of the souls
dance of understandings
of the heart's lingering longing
to touch and be touch
as we wish to belong
with trust receive and given

In this world of deceptions
and mind fuck brilliance
the uncertainty has its place
who and what to trust
in self without doubt
may seem the only respite.

Detachment is key;
yet the paradox lives high
as we are creatures of connection
it is like the air we breathe
and the water we sip
a necessity with little option.

Near or far
there is not difference
as the hearts connection
and souls are one

by choice of music and dance of night

Once connection mixes
its presence be a part of you
as memories or chance
it may fade or linger tight
especially the blessings are known
in the love or fear
it makes little difference
this will continue

As hearts beat rhythms
move the soul to the essence
of the souls knowing of lessons
we all continue the dance
among the stars and galaxies
no matter what the appearance
may be

Relax, enjoy the human experience
just remember…
those you have touched
touch you back
in love or fear
of loss or inspiration
your effects are endless
so be wise
with your actions, thoughts and dances.

Scintillating Dreams

Full moon beaming
Scintillating me
Thoughts of you and all your dreams
Dreams of you and me
Now was it just the dream for you
Was I just the midnight fantasy?
A moment's entertainment and that's all
Connection deep
Distance far
Hearts still met
With music, laughter and the love
Was it all just a game?
Your words were playing
Caused misunderstanding, yet why?
Special mystery and the magic shared…
The changing of your limitations
Now keeps me at bay.
One moment you want me to wait
For what you weren't quite clear.
Change your mind after my reply…
Explain why wait for a friend? And for a year?
I am here and always have been.
So go inquire and find yourself
Until you are willing to meet face to face
And stop the dance you prance…
We are exactly all I can take
Friends in distance and
The rest lives in the silence.

Still questioning what is meant
Give me a call

And we can talk
While the full moon blades across the skies.

Gift from the Mirror

The greatest gift from you was me
You reflected and brought out the best in me
The passions, the drive and an essence of self
From you I also saw my shadow
The games, half truths and dramas
The hidden essence of my brilliance
The mirror of me lives within you
The portions put together
I got the some pieces of the puzzle
As you handed them to me gently
Through the moments of tenderness linger
The vulnerability released and shown
Put a smile on my face and soul
The fighting truths dance inside me
(Tear me up and throw me down
Pick me up and dust me off)
As peace remains and embraces me
As acceptance and allowing happened
Laughing with the deep love that I feel
Through this special connection we know
Now lives inside my heart and Silence
For now we are where we need to be
The longing pulls at me
To share with you at times
As my dreams begins
To live and breathe again.
Wishing for things to be different
With understandings growing within me
As gratitude continues for you
We be friends and support as we can

I am with you and always will
For you are a part of me
Or that is the perception I chose to have
Living in my heart be true
Travel the world and enjoy these truths.

All Good Things in Time

Timing of all good things
Recognized the moment's tender
caress
Gentle essences of the friendship
understood
Release and breath embraced
Love known and unknown passions

Friendships' whispers of the heart
blessed Fingertips touch and keep
moving Knowing the best is what's
deserved. Unknowing the void
created which no one else can fill.
Moonlit dance among the stars brings
peace known

The beauty of the friendship smiling
Within the hearts space growing
Open up to more and expanding
Appreciation for those moment's
treasures
Perhaps another time, maybe not
I be a better person for the moment
I can only hope I left with a smile
remaining
Feeling the connection blessings daily
Timing of all good things
For the gentle essences of friendship
embraced.

Braze of the Midnight Sun

The magic of the midnight sun
Braze, braze...
As friendship denied...

Love still real
Continued passion of sweetest refrain
Till time relives
And painful joy heals.
Silent Silence and highest good...
Dance, dance with the midnight sun
Tantalizing the senses
With realizations

Separation be good for the souls
Hearts beat clear
And opens the door
White Light of Love shared
Between the...

Respect the individual journeys
Seek not, be open
Trust one self and know the other
Stand by, if needed

Regardless of impressions
Silent silence and highest good
Truth of the other and know one self.
The magic of the midnight sun
Braze, braze...
In sweetest demeanor.

Whispering Through the Stars

Shadows dance on the wall
>The mystery of love endure
>Yet actions make certain the reality
>you choosing
>No one loses, nor wins
>Patience is needed.
>Words have power, indeed.
>Passion arises is assured
>When we meet in the silence
>This connection will always exist
>I made peace with this and gained perspective.

>You asked me to keep the poetry alive
>As the words I write embrace you
>Inspiring me with those words of love
>It lives in many forms
>In this warmer place I now call home.
>Again you whisper to me
>Your fears
>Whisper me your passions
>Make peace with me
>And let go of your resistance

>Friction can be fun
>With the right motion
>Embracing and caressing
>Licks and tasting
>Delights in the wonders

>As this friendship and love lives
>It has a life of its own

I embrace it in any form
It takes on dancing within the silence and beyond
As the inspiration it gives me such passion

As I look into the night skies
Seeing your galaxy where ever I be
You be with me
I let you be you where ever you be
Wishing you nearer, yet we will see.
Trust the magic
Trust yourself
Trust me
Trust this connection is pure of heart
And lives within the stars every night.

Telepathic Creations & Creation Be Real

Awoke by the telepathic touch
Within the silence's dance of hearts
Connection distance and seemingly
Once in a while a sign of life
Friendship enduring…
Is this enough?

It is what it is…
I focus on the present day space
All that is happening
Heart centered space and until
time…
Time of more than just a teasing
notion
I let go and let it be.
I reached out and got no reply.
It is what it is
Feeling others and dissolving it all
The space was open in new directions
A voice of realism makes the
difference
No game, conditions…
An open space of discussion
Free of censor; free to be who
And whatever it is.
It is what it is…
And the creation is up to us
Friendship be real, true or just an
illusion
Up to us what the perception it takes
Dissolving the reason why not believe
in the friendship
Trusting the inner knowing and
letting go of ego

Drop the fears and be real…all up to us
Now isn't it?

Hunger Within the Moment's Caress

Standing on the edge of time
The silence surrounding
She feels his presence
His loving essence standing near
Feeling the passion growing
As they have grown in their beingness
With the time shared
Endless yet only this moment exist
As if time is standing still
Yet something is in the way.

She softly whispers to him
Touchez-moi, me reclamer…
He smiles, reaching out…
Taking her firmly in his arms
His lips pressing against hers
Wind of the musing lingers and dances
As their lips taste
The warmth of their beings emerging

The kiss of the moment continues
The passion embracing caress
The songs of their heart melt
Into a beautiful song of adoring bliss.
Heart sings with the eternal dance
Of the lovers knowing trust in each other
And the time together
Nothing else lives in this moment
Yet all is alive and vivid.

Stars shining, brightening the shadows

As the moon fades in the morning's awakening
Skies begin to shake with passion's release
Blissful surrendering of any notions
Heart beat quickens and heats with each
Deeply looking and breathing each other in
Like wine for the sipping, they taste once more
The delightful aroma and flavors lingering
Licking fingertips and other parts
With hungered commotion
Like this is the last meal of this lifetime
Yet knowing this is only the beginning.

devotion music finds

motions
position
emotions
commotion

stillness reigns
the solitude of this devotion
quietude breathes
drinks me in
as if like a glass of fine red wine

music whispers
...come here
come in this sweetness, precious
...dance with me
oh... how can I resist
...damn...
oh this is simply...
music pulls me in
like a finger motioning for me
smiling charm
...damn...

touch my soul
with that delicious moan
..whine..
stillness...silence... divine
oh here I go...
why oh why do I do...
the whisper is so seductive
...damn...
the tenderness

softness of tone
touch me close
stroking the arm
down
down
to the hand
hold by the fingertips
humming…*music* bewitch me
nothing more to say…
…the dance begins…
…so damn…

Sparkles of the Night

Like the sparkles of the night's sky
The twinkling diamonds up in the Heavens
All the possibilities are born
All the wisdoms and fears
Insecurities and Love

Lift up like
…all the multifaceted sides of you
The mask and layers of protection and pain
…Not wanting to hurt

The understandings of existence
Lesson learned, not appreciated
Just examined and tucked away
Behind the mask you wear

Free yourself, Love
Reveal your soul to me
Let loose your inhibition

Come dance with me
Let the rain
P o u r on your s o u l
Purify your mind

Be real and be with me
Shine, shine, shine…
Oh love of my beating heart
Dreams can come true
Believe…

Believe in me
I am real and true for you
Like the stars sparkling in the night's sky

Be-Ness

Take a chance.
Risk…
Be someone who…
Lives.
Be a dancer in the rain, in the sunshine, moonbeams and life.
Life
Be a smile to someone.
Smile.
Be someone who surprises.
Surprise.
Be open.
Open.
Be someone who sings out loud, in tune or not.
Loud
Be the music that moves them.
Move.
Be passionate.
Compassion.
Be a true friend.
True.
Be willing to apologize.
Humble
Be… Breathe deep.
Breathe.
Be unforgettable.
Memorable.
Be real.
Real.

Be Loving.
Love.
Be… Simply Be.
Be.
Be loyal.
Loyal.
Be able to laugh at yourself.
Laughter
Be able to lift someone spirits.
Lifts
Be true to your word.
Word.
Be able to speak your truth and I love you.
Love.
Be there for your friends.
Embrace.
Be creative.
Inspire.
Be true to self.
Self.
Be Love and Loved.
Be.
Be you.
YOU.
Risk lives life smile surprise open loud
Move compassion true humble.
Breathe memorable real love.
Be loyal, laughter lifts word.
Love embrace inspire Self.
Be You.

Spoon

She licked
….the spoon
Slowly…
Embracing the sapidity
Oh my…*whispered under her breath*
Eyes closing with the indolence
Mmmm …
In the delicious delights
dancing…
Passion released!
The flavors teased her
Taste buds and senses
Feeling the smoothness
Sensing the coolness and **heat**
She paused…
Biting her lower lip
As if this was a sin
Enjoying the offering
Savoring…
Looking, reflecting…
Tantalizing
Oh….***the sweet seduction
into another***
She goes again
Slowly…
With the rhythm of the moment
*Sensitization of the life's
pleasures.*
*Oh Yes…
tasting life can be oh so sweet…*

As the Moments We Shared...

Thoughts of you...

... *Melts...*
As the moment we shared
Scintillating into the cosmos
Of understandings and
unconditional love

Time with you...

... *Dances...*
As the moments we shared
Blending into questions
Of understandings and
unconditional love

Love for you

... *Lives...*
As the moments we shared
Stimulating into reflections
Of the understandings and
unconditional love

Essences from you

... *Breathes...*
As the moments we shared
Aspects into mirrors
Of the understandings and
unconditional love

Thoughts, Time, Love, Essences
... melt, dance, live,
breathe...

The understandings...
                        of
unconditional love
As the moments we share.

Awaken by Love

My heart awoke
In love…

…With Love

Understandings and Nuances
Of Love…

Purity and the Game

The **Passion** and *pain*

Love…
…Truly is ALL.

The Rapture, Bliss and Joy
within one's grasp
Only the fear of ego and its
stubbornness,
Of losing oneself in love…

Untrue ~ One will not.
Love enhances the expression of self.
Fear keeps love at bay

Distance *means nothing to love*
With love… there is no such thing
Men have gone to the end of the world…

For Love

For that person who touches
them so deeply
Nothing will keep them away

95

The one love that makes them a better person

More pain when staying away, in denial or repression...
As their heart aches and in pain
Feeling the distance deepens
until love wins or the soul loses
Better to have loved… right?
Yet it is the fool who resist love…
feel that ache forever more…
…with wondering and yearning…

Love… Truly is ALL
Passion and **pain**
Purity and game
Truth of self in the highest form
The highest gain… Love.
I awoke today

In love… with Love…
With all the paradoxically bewilderments.
…blessed be…
That romantic in me.

The Subtle Dreams Motions

The subtle dreams and perception dance
Witness.

Wisdom in the nuances
    of the moment divine.

The subtle dreams and perspectives
Embrace.

Caress the seldom reality
    for the truth unrevealing.

The subtle dreams and presence…
Smile.

Enjoy the touch
   Within the heart beat of oneness.

The subtle dreams and light…
Beaming.

Moon shines and sun light brings all
    into the colours of splendor.

The subtle dreams and passionate…

Love.

Be in the now moment of joy
And allow the acceptance of all to
be.

How Many Ways

how many ways…
can one person cry, feel
and yet simply be?

how can a person who gives…
bleed without end
still continue on
with little more
than a dream

dream…
that is hope
yet not delusion
of its truth

unable to understand
the cruelty
of people to another

being…
friend,
fiend,
family,
or foe

it is a person
with a soul
that dream
that hope
and truth

now with this world
at war within itself
no mind
and little more
than rage

Where is that love
that is all that is?
Where is that love…
where hope lives?

Where kindness
and compassion still lives?
The words of Rumi,
Emerson,
Yeats
and Keats

Of passion,
Of romance
and devotion
to one other.

Where word means something
and keep with trust
honored
and respect

Where one looks out for the
other
Friend is friend
Not just a game
Loyalty lives,
breathes
and true

Make peace
within oneself

Be the person
who is all
one can be

Respect your self,
your dreams,
your soul,
your passions
and friends…

Make the world a better place
what you know it can be
through your words,
your actions,
and truth.

I, The Mirror

I
Am just
one reflection
of
You...

When you look around
You see 360 reflections
like a house mirrors
Surround
You
Always
In Life or Virally...
one reflection or perhaps more...
Even as you look
Into
An actual mirror
You...
You can see
The beauty... The beast...
The artist...The writer...
The narcissist... Introvert...
Exhibitionist...
???

What essence of you
Am I of you?
Love... Fear... Denial... Anger
Passion... Compassion...
Light... Dark... Ego... Heart
???

What mirror am I to you?
Inspiration… Love… Hate
Music… Art… Poetry
Betrayal… Ego…
Heart… Spirit… Truth…Trust
Deception… Dance
???

All are YOU…
REAL
Not just imagination or dream
Not just fantasy or illusion
I live, breathe, real, be…
Like YOU.

You attract me into your world
for a deep understanding of YOU
with
acceptance, allowing,
truth unhidden… revealed.
There is no dismissing…
without your awakening and
awareness
of one thing.

YOU

Simple the truth of You.
I am…
… just one reflection as
You
are just one reflection of…
ME.

Embracing Souls...
Words of the Heart

Words flow into the space of voice
Tone takes shape while mingling with music
Allowing the deeper meaning of connection
As accepting the presence of being to live...

Acknowledgements:

Thank you.
Consider Yourself Hugged,
Loved and Appreciated.

> My family
> My friends
> close and far
> for a moment or a lifetime.
>
> My Inspirations:
> Richard Buhn
> Sy Whitehall
> "the musician"
> Spirit/Source/Creator
> Mother Goddess
> Father God

Blessings to all. You Rock.

Jennifer Hillman,
Writer/Blogger/Poet,
Intuitive Life Coach, Healer

Jennifer Hillman, a born educator, certified life coach and psychic adviser, Jenn Hillman recognized her calling while attending elementary school where she overcame a speech and learning disability (dyslexia). She uses writing to heal and overcome her limitations.
Besides her natural gifts of clairvoyance, clairaudience, clairsentience, empathy, and channeling/medium-ship, Jenn has accumulated other certifications and licenses to offer the most guidance and assurance to her clients. She continues her education to best service herself and her clients. Jen lives in the moment and travels a lot. She works on her professional projects including her company *Jennifer Hillman, Inc* doing business as Angels Intuition, *Inner Strength Coaching*, Abstract Illusions and Abstract Illusions Media. Jen is also a published writer and poet ("Embracing Souls: Poetry of the Dance, Volume I"), and is published on her blogs, Jenn Hillman Reflections and Words of the Soul, as well as published under her pen name on The Rebelle Society and Making Love to Her.

She has a radio program, "Abstract Illusion Radio" or AIR on WolfSpiritRadio.com and other networks. Original programs are recorded on Tuesdays at 9am -11am pacific standard time.

Book Cover:

The cover was designed by Jennifer Hillman, using the sculpture, *"Soul Mates"* a commissioned piece by artist Robert Holmes for Jennifer Hillman.

Jennifer Hillman has been granted exclusive rights to use the sculpture and images for the Embracing Souls Series.

(c)Robert Holmes 2003-present "Soul Mates"

Some Reviews about Words of the Heart:

Words of the Heart is an appropriate title for Jennifer Hillman's book. As I read her poetry, I am encompassed in her world of joy, pain, unconditional love, friendship as well as the love of everything that "is" as well as the comfort of embracing what is yet to come – the reality of the unknown. Her artistic poetry is music to my senses.
 ~Georgiann Kiricoples, Author of *The Soul's Bridge;* Internet Radio Host of *Breaking Through* with Georgiann; Founder and owner of Kirico Inc.

I have always felt a certain connection with Jennifer and after reading her poetry book "Words of the Heart" it was reaffirmed by the content of her poems.
Being the Author of *It's Monday Only in Your Mind* has afforded me the opportunity to get a first hand look at Jennifer's work and I found many similarities in my book which mirrors her poems, the difference being, in her book life is expressed so beautifully in the language of poetry. Through her poems she touched my soul. The core of life itself is love and she captures love's

expression in many different ways in vivid detail in her poetry. I would recommend this book to anyone. To me it expresses the majesty of life in the form words. It is an honor and privilege to be on this journey of life with her. With the way Jennifer's heart is aligned with Universal Love, her work has already and will bring much more satisfaction to our world.
~ Michael Cupo, Author of *It's Only Monday in Your Mind.*

"Words of the Heart are exactly what Jennifer Hillman delivers in this collection of poems. The imperative theme that *we all are one* and a *reflection of each other* is emphasized and restated throughout the book. Jennifer's uplifting spirituality is contagious and well worth your time and treasury."
~Charles Redner, Publisher, *The Hummingbird Review*

When reading poetry like Jennifer Hillman writes, it's difficult to put a description of it into words. Her verses are like a softly spoken voice; they feel almost like a light breeze does on my skin. Yet there is nothing fragile about this voice. On the contrary, beneath the sensitivity is a powerful voice. One of wisdom, grace and strength. A visionary. A voice that can reach out and touch souls. Sooth. Uplift. Guide. This is poetry that speaks the language of emotion, reaching down to the very core of essential being. If Love had a language, it would be "Words of the Heart".
~Linda May Kallestein, *Kallestein Publishing*

Words of the Heart are Jennifer Hillman's words *from* the heart; an expression of divinity straight from the Source of divinity.
~Matthew J. Pallamary, Author of *Land Without Evil* and *Spirit Matters*

www.ingramcontent.com/pod-product-compliance
Lightning Source LLC
LaVergne TN
LVHW021400080426
835508LV00020B/2381